Artistic Poetry

Brian D Ball

Grosvenor House
Publishing Limited

This book is published by
Grosvenor House Publishing Ltd
Link House
140 The Broadway, Tolworth, Surrey, KT6 7HT.
www.grosvenorhousepublishing.co.uk

This book is a work of fiction. Any resemblance to
people or events, past or present, is purely coincidental.

A CIP record for this book
is available from the British Library

ISBN 978-1-80381-044-7

ACKNOWLEDGEMENTS

GROSVENOR HOUSE   for their support and advice

ALMA EVANS   My personal MENTOR

PETER COX   Local Poet

LARRY LARSEN   Local musician

INDEX

CREATIVE MIND

A creative notion,
fearful and frightening,
breaking my heart,
resentment and desolation,
splitting my brain in half.
Passions I want today,
words cracking my soul,
firing across the bleak desert,
sand pouring out of my mouth.
Trying to write stories as if true,
mind confused and bewildered,
brawling with my inner thoughts.
Reality striving to disappear,
lacking in rhythm and lyrics,
sound pounding within.
My heart beating fast and slow,
attempting to find new stories,
peoples' personal enhanced opinions,
pain anguishing with love,
inside my creative mind.
A war rallying around my veins,
shaking until the last word
and the save button is pressed.

READING A STORY

Book I can't put down,
pages I continue to turn,
paper smelling of mould,
smooth and musty to handle.
Fingers sticky and sweaty,
arms working like labourers,
eyes red and shimmering,
cheeks blush nervously.
Story enhancing the brain,
soaking my senses
drowning the thoughts.
My body shaking consistently,
emotions unsettled throughout,
a shiver penetrating the mind.
Story I believe is true.
Book I can't put down.

MEN IN TIGHTS

Amateur dramatics my only fame,
show standing out in my brain.
Women I played looking insane.
I wore lipstick, a bright red flame.
My snow white face giving me a stage name.
A wig as long as a freight train
and a short skirt revealing knees like a marine.
Wearing two artificial breasts, not a mark retained,
high heels making me walk as if with a frame.
Putting tights on was a different domain,
dreading a continuous pain.
Slow at first needing a glass of champagne,
curling up inside toes like a snake wanting to maim.
Then trying at speed as if in the fast lane,
making my tights rip revealing my naked skin.
Eventually some success I shout in vain,
for males they are not designed.
Only women can wear tights and still smile.

THE CREATIVE ARTIST

The artist studies the view.
A gate coloured in a dirty blue.
Nearby a shoe standing like a statue,
close to a small stream as damp as dew
and an upside down boat with paint peeling too.
Clouds he imagines as a zoo,
only he can see a kangaroo.
He mixes his paint like a stew,
sticking to pad like glue
and passed onto the canvas like a stage crew.
Paint runs down his clothing as if he's got the flu.
He paints the shoe entering the gate so blue,
the inner story he tries to pursue,
hoping it is studied by quite a few.
All concentrating on the shoe,
hoping owner opens gate and goes through.

THE PICTURE

Reds, greens, and yellows sparkle,
within the frame of the visionary,
erupting on canvas and sounding lyrical,
making the painting feel topical.
The colours revolving around squares and circles,
as if the painting is becoming theatrical,
producing an imaginary structure,
helping to create a fictional story.
Whites and blacks making the picture look physical,
creating shapes that are four dimensional,
so human figurines can look logical
and stride towards a brightly coloured obstacle,
which makes them look real and very magical.
We study the picture, which is classical,
then draft a poem about the painting's potential
and everyone's tale is extremely individual.

FLOWING STREAM

Sun reflecting off the water,
shadows looking unnatural,
alien lights bouncing,
stream trying to surge,
rocks stopping motion,
attempting a graceful flow.
Drifting across valley,
like snakes crawling laterally,
or ants following their leader,
confused by a twig or two,
stopping them going onwards,
baffling their mechanical minds.
A mythical thought prevailing,
artists dreaming of view,
photo looking like a painting,
scenery looking unreal.
The stream on a sinuous journey,
around valley of my heart.

PAINTED FLOWER

Flowers painted softly,
colours amalgamating,
sagging in the middle,
peeling from the edges.
Flaking inwardly within.
An alien travelling through veins,
securing passion and desire,
smell sweetly scented,
soaking all my heart.
Dream that is true,
story of godly facts,
petal landing in the water,
lovers swimming in the lake,
mirror on the shiny surface
naked, vulnerable and desirable.
Mythology of love.
Life of happiness.

VAN GOGH'S CAFE

I look at the painting.
Buildings with shutters,
empty balcony above.
Shapes irregular.
Chairs are uniform,
raised above cobbles.
Sky sparkles like spaceships,
looking down on ladies,
dressed to impress.
I stand and linger,
studying one girl,
sitting alone and sad,
with flowing dress.
I ask wanting to join.
She says yes.
We enjoy tea together
like lifelong friends,
but her name I don't know.
We walk to her home,
down cobbled streets,
where she lives alone,
share Champagne,
spend night together.
It's only a painting.
I'm sat on my own.

LOVE ON A RUBBISH HEAP

My heart is bouncing,
cracking under pressure,
swaying within the rubbish,
fluctuating the historical items.
Emptiness where once was full,
a bag that once was packed,
chickens burnt to the bone,
cabbage left uneaten.
Love tilting towards the middle,
waiting patiently with optimism,
climbing to the top of the heap,
looking over the clouds.
My body shaking with fear,
vibrating through my layers,
snake wrapping herself around me,
squeezing and soaking my soul.
Rubbish thoughts are dominant,
love will return I am confident.
Fire a bullet into the atmosphere,
stop it landing inside my psyche.

ABRACADABRA

Disappearing without trace.
Assisted by his magic wand,
hey-presto she's gone,
breaking my heart,
mindful of the past.
Happiness was the word.
Now tears flow down my face,
wanting love again,
seeing her blue eyes,
blooming cheeks,
sparkling covered legs.
Only yesterday I smiled,
hugged her as if mine.
He's waved his wand,
taking her away,
making her disappear for good.

PAIN OF LIFE

My heart pounding, pain releasing,
percussion performer, wanting to please,
rhythm escaping, grief covering face,
uncomfortable, painful and embarrassing.
Boxer losing fight, winning people's sympathy,
cash easing pain, making pride less upsetting.
Unpleasant around mouth, dry crusty and scarred,
open and visible, afraid of a volcanic eruption,
petrified of snake curling up inside my throat,
knowing the outcome, however much it hurts.
Love I still have, emotion burning within,
eyes bursting open, tears flowing down face,
a slow narrow stream trickling down body,
dreading what's ahead, fearful of future,
now we have parted, going our own way.

FIRE WITHIN THE HEART

Emotions firing through veins,
straining feelings with pain,
portraits of lovers insane,
showing the heart of design,
flying through the body like an airline.
Love and passion combined,
joined together completely entwined,
affection never once declined.
Firing through the life of humankind,
live fireworks blowing in the wind,
brain exploding towards Mastermind,
feelings completely outshined.

NEW LOVERS GOING HOME

New lovers leaving the bar at closing time,
underground station they are trying to find,
both giggling to keep in a straight line.
Find a train and seats for their desires,
feeling claustrophobic and emotional,
they continue to sit in their own shrine.
Two lovers stuck together tightly and bound,
with their lips bulging and round,
they whisper a quiet rhyme,
fulfilling cravings within their minds.
Their brains filled with passion
and their souls fragmenting like twine,
touching closely as if they are on their own.
In the tube they travel alone,
travelling towards her home.
Their first time as new lovers.

HEALTHY DESIRE

I'm walking without knowing,
lingering without thinking,
my mind wandering and dreaming,
truth I am starting to believe.
I stand hoping for an answer,
upright and determined like a professor,
eyes focused on the dancer,
ears listening for correctness.
Romantically I look at her gestures,
wanting to study her physical structure,
softly touching her body all over.
We smile as if we are content,
kissing while feeling confident.
Our faces covered in lipstick like paint.
Lovers we are starting to become.

DIAMOND RING

It's pureness touching the heart with vigour,
drawing the subject, enhancing the figure,
imaginary magnet connecting the finger,
where naked pulses continue to linger,
the diamond fires towards the spiritual singer.
Resembling a vibrant museum exhibit
or a bright laser beam with no limit.
The women's ring is a pure winner,
given by her adoring partner,
like a poem written on the wing
before a song is romantically sung in spring.
She sees her finger covered,
a bright pure diamond discovered.

ONE SOCK

We wash the clothes making them clean,
which makes the old ones look new
and soap sticks to the fabrics like glue.
Socks enter as lovers do,
into the washing machine two by two,
trying hard not to be alone.
Though one sock seems to roam,
disappearing like a magical moonstone,
leaving other in the machine on its own
so it finishes up completely marooned.
The lost sock we hope will return home,
as we join them together as one,
keeping my feet warm on a winter's afternoon.

WALKING ON MY OWN

Dark and cold night,
long country lane,
rain pouring, not thinking.
Hammer gently hitting floor.
Dog barking.
Strange noises,
birds, chickens, even ghosts,
scary sounds of insects,
making my hair curl.
I can't tell a soul,
on my own,
but not sure,
think I am being stalked,
by rain following me,
making me wet.
Rain running down me,
cuddling up close,
romantically touching my heart.

HOT, HUMID AND WET

It's baking hot, humid and damp.
Heart shrinking and feeling wet,
water soaking within a naked soul,
bombarding the thought process,
wet, sticky and sweaty,
continuous water flowing,
like Niagara Falls in slow motion.
Clothes itching, wanting to strip,
veins tickling as they drift through body,
feeling bedraggled, scruffy and bemused.
Walking slowly through the haze,
wanting to sleep until it cools,
dreaming of snow.

NO SOCKS NEEDED

Weather clammy and muggy,
scorching tropical heat,
sweat looking like a reservoir,
faster than a burst dam,
damper than the ocean.
Clothes removed with friction,
peeling from scorched bodies.
Sound of ripping and tearing,
no ruptures or splitting,
Velcro sticking, but not working.
With bare feet we are walking,
across rough and ragged terrain.
Shorts dirty and torn,
rest of me naked and red raw.
Thinking of wasted shopping time,
upstairs in M&S next to undies,
deciding what socks to buy.

LOST

Lost in the desert,
rivers dry and musty,
craters large but arid,
view a lifetime away.
My head spinning; crowds cheering;
tall attractive ladies flirting,
long naked legs touching mine,
loads of money flying,
heading in my direction,
looking at gold, teasing my soul.

Head stops spinning, no one stares,
money has flown away,
ladies not teasing me anymore.
Left me in a room all on my own.
Wallet empty no more gold.
Lost at roulette.
Lost in the desert.

DESERT TRAVELLER

Travelling across the wilderness,
sand firing into the air.
Spring heading towards heaven,
water pretending to be there,
dust elevating within,
soaking my inner eye,
baking and burning the skull,
fireball touching and exploding.
The mind skims across the surface,
fluctuating the heartbeat,
making me gasp for air.
Travelling across time zones,
confusing my thought process,
making me stutter and mutter,
frightening and exciting me together.
Penetrating my inspirations,
thoughts making me feel flat like a puncture,
trying to stop me going forward,
making sure I don't go back.

LAND'S END TO
JOHN O' GROATS

Sun hot, sky blue, skin red.
People wave as I leave,
shouting to someone close,
unfortunately, not myself.
Continue across weathered rocks,
noise of the sea the only sound,
volume increasing as it hits the edge,
enhanced by seagulls just above.
Some birds disappearing,
floating into the mysterious sea cave,
sounding like babies trapped in their cots.
I turn and follow the ragged path,
passing and admiring the lifeboat station.
I reach the magical Sennen Cove,
with gift shops illuminating the sky,
like a scene from a nursery rhyme.
Then I join the semi-naked people
trying to get a tan on the sand.
Yes, I have done the walk.
Walked from Land's End to the cove,
a dream in my mind that won't leave.
John O' Groats another year.

ABANDONED IN HAYLE

Sun bleaching the dunes,
grass absorbing the heat,
greens of different shades,
growing out of the sand,
rising towards the sky
with chalky white reflections.
Softly my bare feet are immersed,
silent, eerie and spine chilling,
a desert running into the sea,
waves flexing muscles for power.
Occasional semi-nude bodies,
laying like brown corpses,
without any movement,
the heat burning their souls.
Seagulls breaking the silence,
gathering food from the water,
while the fish carry on as normal,
not knowing their outcome.
The sand dunes stretch for miles,
absorbing spiritual feelings.
The ghosts of the vast oceans
visit Hayle for a day.

BLUE DOOR

Street lights in St. Ives our only visibility.
A ghost walk, without hostility,
arrives at shining blue door looking blissful,
terrace house old and peaceful.
It's current owner proud of the property.
Our guide whose thick beard is graceful,
is a storyteller who stares with eyes glazed,
at door in an extremely scary way
wondering about the unusual eerie tale.
'A man walks in without turning yale,
the windows locked looking frail,
and making it stranger as he came by rail,
he purchased it as an empty shell,
but later, sold it in a sad sale.'
House empty as the owner is in jail,
and previous owner's dead, wearing a veil.
We wait for the ghost to reappear.

CAPTAIN'S LAST VOYAGE

It has been a long sea journey,
but think it's near the end.
The ship's hull soaking up the tide.
Everyone's tired and bedraggled,
long time since leaving America,
with our cargo of gin.
Alcohol keeping us sane is running dry,
fights and arguments breaking out on board.
Sails are making a noise like a bird,
only made when near land,
not heard for months, maybe more.
Families will be waiting ashore,
to hug and great us all.
Flashing lights brightly visible,
seeing home, we start to smile.
Sails are lowered gently.
Most of us start to wave.
Then a jolt making us shake,
followed by a silent pause,
fear felt by all on board,
realising we are in Cornwall,
long way from home.
We have been fooled by pirates,
our deaths the only outcome.

CAR ON THE SCRAP HEAP

I am a car, sad and bewildered,
feeling rejected and shattered,
my bodywork scratched and tattered,
trying to grin and not be deterred.
As a car remembering good like a wizard,
trips on boats forward and windward,
especially fun during a blizzard.
Pride I felt when my owner graduated,
driving on his own he was delighted,
better still with girlfriend, so devoted.
When I collided, he felt dejected,
making me feel disjointed.
I feel happy after being altered,
like a female mechanic feeling weird,
a student making me feel elevated,
but I am getting old and dilapidated,
MOT test the paperwork says failed.
Looking back feeling appeased.
Will I go to heaven? Or am I being conceited?

BOY'S TOY

Driveway steep making an incredible picture.
Excitement as we enter as two lovers,
on the edge of Snowdon making our minds wonder,
visiting lover's godfather at our leisure,
a sit-on train set in garden, a marvellous fixture.
We ride on his train only stopped by buffers,
with excitement as if we are pulling crackers.
My eyes popping with glitter,
me a boy in a man's container
and my brain rising as if it's on an elevator.
We ride around on the train as if we are visionaries.
On a train dreaming we have surrendered,
over viaduct and through tunnels all miniature,
past stations made of timber,
looking at models of people covered in plaster.
I have a turn at being the driver,
giving me power that I want for ever.
Then we are called to the mansion,
which is covered in heather.
Food is ready and we are told to stay together,
joined by the lady and gentlemen of the manor,
surrounded by portraits of their ancestors.

SAD TRAIN OF WINDSOR

Old and creaky.
Remembering the past,
excitement when new.
Journeys I completed,
through cities, busy,
bustling with people.
Countryside silent,
birds singing pleasantly.
Boats softly moored.
Train finishing at terminals;
cathedrals of lavishness.
Through day, night,
clouds, sunshine,
rain and snow.
I look back and cry,
gazing at the river,
the hectic town,
castle above the station.
Only a branch line,
heading for retirement,
on a single track.

TRAIN TRAVELLING
THROUGH TUNNEL

The rock creeps nearer,
train nearly touching,
daring me to peep.
Darkness makes me perspire.
Can't help peering,
feeling the wind,
making cheeks ache.
Look towards front,
surprise hits me hard,
light pulling me in,
like a mystical man,
purifying my heart.
Quick as a tiger,
train leaves tunnel,
blinding my thoughts.

RUSH HOUR (LONDON)

People bustling,
lots of bodies jostling,
showing visible muscle,
in train under tunnel.
Doors open, everyone stumbles,
no one tumbles,
lots moan and grumble,
trying to be humble.
Through door at an acute angle,
squeezed like a mangle,
strangers you want to strangle,
pushing and getting in a tangle,
outside light as bright as a candle,
narrow ray a blinding dazzle.
People trying to manhandle,
while looking puzzled,
escaping with slight shuffle,
walking into a puddle,
colliding and touching knuckles.
In a city without air bubbles.
A city where no one sleeps.

UNDER LONDON

Sweat and tears,
push and flow,
holding onto other peoples' bodies.

Suits, jackets, ties and trousers,
soaking wet and smelly.
Girls with tattoos all over their bodies,
and the men's faces covered too.
Pins in noses, breasts and other painful places.
People black, white, green and yellow.

Everyone is going somewhere,
some unsure of what they'll find.
But we are under London and no one cares.

CAMDEN GOTHS

Fluorescent bodies glitter,
rushing as if there is no tomorrow.
Camden awash with perspiration.
Faces, non-descript white,
arms, legs, naked skin too.
Girls' lipstick dark black.
Bodies pierced, tattoos of ghosts.
Shoes black, dark and dreary.
Through Camden I walk,
past their ghostly apparitions,
looking for Costas to have a coffee.

BOURNEMOUTH CLOSED

Sand, several shades of orange.
Deckchairs covered,
waiting for fat ladies
to undress and reveal their skin.
Freshly painted beach huts,
brightly coloured and empty,
drawers with no spare knickers.
Pier vacant and tranquil,
where a few walk in the breeze.
Zip wire waiting for the brave.
Cafe unoccupied and depressed,
smelling of wet paint,
not sticky buns and coffee.
Gift shops with no fancy goods,
shelves daring people to touch,
paint turning individuals white not brown.
Everyone hoping for scorching summer.
Money spent without thought.

ROOM WITH NO VIEW

Private, compact, dirty and black,
peeling fragments and flaking paint,
windowless, dark and gloomy.
He sits in solitude and misery,
shared with insects, mice and flies
all trying to keep warm.
Newspapers replacing stylish carpets,
boxes substituting tables with fancy designs,
blankets instead of beds made by Ottoman,
clothes torn, bedraggled and dirty.
Lots of alcohol to avoid hunger,
drugs to keep him sane.
No fitted kitchen from Ikea.
Sharp designed bedrooms not for him.
Electricity and gas a thing of the past,
no television to keep him happy;
EastEnders, Emmerdale and Casualty.
Just one room, condemned and depressing,
with no windows for light.

HOME SWEET HOME

On a street and homeless,
with all his possessions,
a brown box his luxury bed,
no springs to ease the pain.
Newspapers with yesterday's news,
keeping him warm on frosty nights.
Alcohol relaxing the soul,
making him smile and laugh.
Drugs so he can dream alone,
of a starter home of his own,
with door to his small castle for self-esteem,
and bed upstairs in little room,
overlooking a square lawn,
with wardrobe for clean and warm clothes,
not garments bedraggled and badly torn.
But still on the street and begging,
pride reduced to a single heartbeat.
Living like an animal in the wild,
existing by eating unwanted scraps.
Laying down unable to stand,
hoping one day things will change.

BUILDING EMPTY AND SAD

Looking through eyes invisible but clear.
The building glitters without shine,
the bar empty and dry.
Inside dirty and dull, cobweb trapping flies,
who scream and unscripted they slowly die.
Spiders wait for comedy to return,
laughter and smiles to fill the auditorium again.
Ghostly comedians waiting with apprehension,
frantically enter stage to applause and laughter,
only enjoyed by the non-living with smiling faces.
Outside building is sad, comedy sign falling,
missing many letters, front door boarded,
colourful hoardings gone, sparkling no more.
Sky looking glum, moon full of tears,
no voices projecting far, building with no echoes,
comedy and laughter are the building's history.

MY SHED

Open door, cannot see floor,
shove box aside.
Hammer falls missing me by a hair,
excited chisel jumps, bouncing off toe,
alarming rake knocking me against bucket
that I thought was empty.
Axe flies towards me,
misses, but scatters nails and screws on base,
piercing my bare feet, blood spurts out.
In pain I re-install box.
Slam door shut.

MAY I COME IN
FOR A CUP OF TEA

Your place looks gorgeous!
I looked through your window,
the design is imposing,
making mine ordinary.
Your garden is outstanding!
The design makes mine bland.
Your kitchen is superior!
The colours are majestic.
Your clothes are nice.
Friends look wild.
You never pull your curtains,
so I can't help but see.

May I come in for a cup of tea?
That's not kind what you said.
All I want is to look.
I can't help being nosy.

LOG BURNER

Centre of room the log burner stands.
Noise of hitchhikers rustling paper dry.
Shadow trembles while wall teases fly.
The flue reaching for heaven to spy.
We sit in our underwear looking at sky.
Inside television tries to prioritize.
We stare at box with our snake eyes,
trying not to study and analyse.
Body glued, face galvanized.
Log burner flashes and electrifies,
trying to make heat intensify.
Look at painting, feeling mesmerised,
envision visiting paradise.
Dream I am there to my surprise,
thinking of a holiday with delight.
Get a brochure to entice.
Listen to log burner being hypnotised.

THE COUNTRY PUB

Walk to the pub which is upstream
and enter at speed, hitting my brow on the beam,
stand by the wooden bar, polished so it gleams.
A drink I need to celebrate my winning team.
The head on my beer looks like cream,
pouring down the side like a stream.
Beer spills over me as if I am the victim,
looking like I have been for a swim,
making alcohol run down my skin.
The floor of the pub looks like an aquarium.
Nuts on the bar give us protein.
Drunken sweaty bodies make it fill like a solarium
and always stay the same whatever millennium.
I wish I had been to the football stadium.

LEAVING PUB

Shut door of pub,
march along road,
arms and legs out far
in a stately deliberate manner,
to a rhythm loud and clear,
only we can hear,
soldiers on parade.
Our red faces restoring pride.
Walking down long lane,
in unaccustomed surroundings,
making us fall into hedge,
faces covered in mud,
camouflaged ready for war,
heading for unknown house,
all sleeping in rows,
fully clothed, feeling ill,
in unfamiliar barracks.
Next day wake slowly,
head spinning and lost.
Leaving for home feeling unwell,
where wives and girlfriends wait,
capturing us like the enemy,
in prison in our own homes,
ordered to work like slaves.

DRUNK - I AM DRUNK

Alcohol creating voices louder than a hound,
making eyes imagine we are fogbound
and difficult to walk on flat ground.
Lost although I am in my home town,
wanting to sleep but have no nightgown,
confused, incomplete and having a meltdown.
I am persistently acting like a circus clown,
with face colour of red and wanting to frown,
when speaking, I cannot find a noun.
My head feels too big for a crown,
thinking of myself as someone of renown,
meaning my alcoholic excesses have let me down.
I fall into a stream where I nearly drown,
making my body a dirty brown,
and regretting having that last ale.

BREAKING GLASS

Crystal glass shattering,
echoing and vibrating,
scattering all over the floor.
Pieces all in miniature,
crunching and crumbling,
sounding like cymbals
out of tune and cold.
It is swept almost clear,
daring people to walk,
however harmful.
Bare feet we walk.
It laughs at us,
knowing the truth,
it's not completely gone.
It attacks our naked skin,
causing blood to squirt,
painting floor red.
Broken glass will go,
clear and safe for a time,
bare feet we can walk.

BAR STOOL

At bar with a beer.
Barmaid leaning and peering.
I do the same and stare.
My girlfriend kicks me firmly,
we both laugh and squeal,
drinking several more beers.
Music loud but cannot hear,
both entwined, lovers touching.
Bar full of bric-a-brac,
that we don't see or care.
Just fondle close and cuddle,
thinking we are completely alone,
lips succulently touching tenderly,
on an island far from home.

A dream while laying facing ceiling,
waking up ready for another day,
rush around and get prepared.
Windows sealed shut,
held captive behind bars,
sitting on my own,
speaking to lover on phone.

EMPTY AND SILENT

Trains running empty.
Cities no people.
Shops closed and vacant.
Silent, still and bleak.
Flamboyantly eerie and scary.
Painted restaurants smelly,
feeling robustly miserable,
their cookers lonely and gloomy,
ghosts the only customers,
money they have none.
Car's static, batteries powerless,
breakdown service waiting,
trees tingling their bonnets,
hoping for seduction.
Locals walking and exercising,
nervously keeping a distance,
carrying tapes two metres long,
lovers blowing kisses,
waiting to cuddle again.

LONELY COWBOY

The cowboy rides into town,
dust billowing as he turns,
dirty smell he's reeking,
the only company a lonely rattlesnake.
Grime creates a dusty saddlebag,
garments dirty, only used as rags,
hat swathed in dust making it sag,
boots making feet sore and haggard.
Eyes focussed on bar so he can brag.
Hotel door not ajar, no cigars.
Despondent notice on door,
sign saying bar is closed today.
Two metres apart you must be.
No fighting to get local girls.
No one in the empty street.
No lady to give him a treat.
No sizeable evening banquet.
No one carrying out gun fights.
No room in the inn for cowboy.

I DON'T WANT TO
BE A COWBOY

Being a gold digger is my dream,
going west to succeed,
to get rich then influential,
paying for girls' services with gold.
Buildings empty when arriving,
no one in dusty township.
Hotel deserted, paint peeling,
nowhere to clean the naked soul,
the gold not shining anymore.
I continue west by horse,
my trusted life time friend.
Outside town meet a real cowboy,
who teaches me all I need to know,
where to find girls who take cash.
I became the fastest cowboy in the west.

HE RIDES INTO TOWN

Cowboy rides into town,
hat on head revealing frown,
only one thing on his mind,
kill Johnny so he is side-lined,
and bleeds so much he drowns.
In front of building, the cleanest in town,
doors stylish and renowned.
Wind blowing bar sign down,
creaking and echoing around,
and drunks laying on ground.
Lady standing without sound,
hair extended and blonde,
long white dress flowing beyond,
grey, dirty and torn.
He descends from horse to reach out,
walking towards her hoping to bond,
and in love hoping for a response.
Kiss and embrace without remorse,
no need to change course,
like a laser firing towards source.
Everyone knows no killing today.
That's how Johnny became best man
at the wedding of the year.

LONG WALK

Weather cloudy, humid and hot.
I am not yet ten years old,
and been playing with friends.
Turn and walk down alley long,
on my own as all have gone.
I see my dad upright and straight,
next to him my cat at attention,
both looking anxious.
I wonder if it is the garage,
collapsed in pieces on the floor.
Mum joked it would one day.
A wooden structure leaning over to the right.
Looking forward I continue down drive,
high walls making it seem further.
I want to get there rapidly,
but ages it seems to take.
When I arrive, I see the fear.
My cat jumps touching my face,
licking me and covering me with saliva.
My dad's face shows concern,
he opens his mouth and speaks:
    "Your grandad is dead".

MY PROUD GRANDAD

He walked as if in the military,
his trilby hat my main memory.
Was told he was working class in the factory,
though not agreeing, but replying bravely,
that all should be treated equally.
Others disagreed and dressed traditionally,
with flat caps and overalls for machinery.
My nan and grandad lived in harmony,
sitting in their armchairs using correct crockery,
loving each other's company.
He was proud of the monarchy,
but most of all proud of his family.
To me he was never ordinary
and I wish I could be his contemporary.

MY DNA IS ALIEN

My nan's distant grandmother,
twenty and dressed as a sculpture,
a virgin not looking to the future.
Then naked, with doors ajar,
joined by an alien on his first endeavour,
instruction manual not familiar,
pressure forcing his essence inside.
Not sure of outcome.
Not sure how.

STAGE TWO

Inside her pregnant body,
baby is gesturing directly,
getting restless and anxious.
Half alien, half human not visible,
trying to learn his mother's status.
Irresistible urge forcing him to exit.
Not sure of outcome.
Not sure how.

STAGE THREE

He's neither alien nor human,
giving him a unique foundation,
hair thick will always be an indication,
appendix operation to be actioned.
A new race, a new DNA element,
magnetically forcing confrontation.
Not sure of outcome.
Not sure what's next.

STAGE FOUR

Several generations forward,
I try to explain in words,
the truth I try to assert,
my ancestors past revealed.
Half alien without any doubt,
'my DNA is unique' I rant,
making me a creative student.
Not sure of outcome.
Not sure what's next.

FLASH OF LIGHT

Fireworks firing into orbit,
circling past, then present.
Sky disappearing and eroding,
my pleasant times exploding.
Looking back heart is probing,
regrets some but not moaning,
learning and still growing,
like a rhyme written in a poem.
Dream of holidays golden,
future a brilliant goal.
Life has been a tall pole,
travelling through black holes,
exciting and enjoyable stroll.
Living has never been dull,
fireworks within my soul,
fireworks burning my skull.

THE MOON CRIES AGAIN

Moon looks ordinary,
with craters visible,
it's here for good,
though that won't last.
Then bits fall off
making it scream with pain,
getting louder and louder.
Blood covering the sky,
tears falling from its face,
sobbing vibrating all around.
Size reduces to a fraction,
less when face goes too.
Disappearing completely,
emptiness where once he was.
The shrieking fades,
we mourn his loss.

THE EARTH LOOKS
AT ITSELF

The planet looks through the mirror at itself,
as if it's an X-rated movie picture.
Oceans getting rougher for seafarers,
scary and loud like an orchestra.
Frozen caps watched from a clipper,
ice disappearing the same as clothes from a stripper,
water rising higher observed by the skipper,
then flooding as the earth loses its temper.
Dense gasses bellowing from a steamer,
this carbon dioxide not considered by local planners
which returns to heat the globe making forests smoulder.
I am concerned knowing future generations will suffer,
another Noah's Ark preventing man's destruction,
Hoping ice will return and the world will be covered,
making the Earth spin forever.

RED MORNING SKY

Red stripe strides across sky,
like gentlemen's underwear,
Turner on a blank canvas.
Barbara Hepworth dreaming,
sculptures reaching heaven,
straight and formal.
Not sure if it's spring,
leaves appearing again,
birds singing for us.
Summer is nearly here.

DREAM BEFORE THE STORM

Ideas forcing eruptions in the sky,
burning and piercing the heart,
eyes tense and bewildering
like a ghost capturing and penetrating.
Python teasing the tongue,
spirit regurgitating out of its mouth,
saliva firing into the open air.
Sky scared, tense and frightened,
it's fearful soul anxious and apprehensive.
Devil's hand reaching,
protecting me from pain,
accepting my adultery, lies and sin,
as the truth is red raw within.
Waiting for my punishment,
taking it like a man.

LEAP INTO THE DARK

Helmet is on my head,
the light is switched to bright.
I am hoisted into the dark,
down a hole that's deep,
arriving faster than a tiger,
just my light reflecting in the gloom.
Turn right and my eyes open wide,
brightness competing with the sun.
Stalactites and stalagmites long,
looking out at space and exploring,
gazing at fish swimming without water.
Rocks of different shades of blue,
shining like a Hobbit's castle,
or a cathedral in the lower depths,
waiting for crowds to appear.
But I have got to leave,
turning towards darkness again.

UP TO THE SKY

Climbing to the heights,
heading for the clouds,
which are white and crusty,
I stand on some ragged rocks.
Anxiety gripping my heart as it beats,
ropes tightly under control,
clasping onto a harness,
pretending to be brave,
shaking as if afraid.
Surrounded by wilderness,
relying on others,
imagining I am alone.
Body cold and shivering,
satisfied and proud,
then I reach the peak,
looking down at the view.
On top of the world,
feeling delighted and powerful,
mountain I've captured,
sky I have nearly reached.

TREE REACHES FOR THE SKY

Tree reaching to high elevation,
branches gripping the clouds,
pulling them down from the sky.
Roots aiming for middle earth,
competing with the trolls for food.
Tree drinks the water until dry,
making the trunk expand,
pushing it nearer to the sky,
in a forest without natural light.
The water is struggling to rise,
plants are unable to compete,
worms feeling safe from attack.
Soil is hard for animals to burrow.
Trolls find it difficult to come out to play.

FOREST WITHOUT LIGHT

Looking at the forest and studying,
near or far still muddy,
my brain exhausted feeling fuzzy,
mind confused and fluffy.
Trees heading for heaven like lovers,
branches caressing their neighbours.
Mirage of a creative cave digger,
ghostly, eerie and feeling rickety,
a shadow to make them look guilty.
Forest lights flicker motionless and steady,
changing destination rapidly,
breaking the thought process sharply.
Trees giving the effect of velocity,
screaming and studying botany,
making birds sing their biography.
I continue to look and study.

FOREST

Healthy looking trees,
stems extremely chubby
and looking very bulky,
with branches exceedingly bushy,
surviving until they are elderly.
They stand in mud, which is boggy,
making the ground slippery,
with mushrooms like a picture of broccoli.
Ants invading as an army,
as if from another country,
making the small twigs very slushy,
giving the impression of a fantasy,
or a horror movie.
The branches' eyes look extremely teary,
weeping and looking weary.

MASHED APPLE

Wind blowing, apples falling,
landing on runway, grassed.
Looking up at fruit ripe and content,
feeling rotten and bewildered,
holes implanted, maggots imprinted,
mashed, brown, soggy and bruised.
Sun burning, penetrating fire.
Apple lonely, frightened and tearful.
It's only wanted by animals wild,
deer munching deliberately until gone.
Worms torment apple making them wet,
using their muscular pharynxes to kill.
Birds peck making apples cry.
Hurting the souls of the mashed apples.

HIDDEN SOUL

Tiger with reactive camouflage,
slinking into the wild undergrowth,
waiting patiently and stationary,
feeling wet and sticky.
Tiger lies flat without a sound,
not a thought or a whisper,
trying not to breathe,
movement non-existent,
body curved and ready.
The prey unaware,
running around without a care.
The tiger's back raised firmly,
still no sound or vibration,
waiting for his opportunity.
Tiredness overcomes the prey,
making it vulnerable to attack.
Then the tiger prepares itself,
with its whole body moving,
faster and faster it travels,
dust covering the ground,
a sandstorm exploding.
The tiger grabs its prey,
giving its family food on the table.

GALLOPING HORSE

The stallion is galloping along,
determined and feeling headstrong,
like a rhythm of a train humming a song
and the ground vibrating the same as ping-pong.
The horse's hooves sounding like loud gongs,
as he gallops away from the stable where he belongs,
the distance of which is only a furlong.
He is running around a field that is oblong.
His trainer's dream is totally life long,
that one day he will be like Red Rum,
and race at Aintree and be number one.

THE LONELY,
LONELY HORSE

The sensitive horse,
sad and feeling distraught,
standing isolated and cold,
lonely with no companion,
in a pasture of mud.
Grass a long time gone,
only hay for food,
munching, teeth crackling.
An eye gazing in thought,
tears trickle down face,
oozing like melting ice,
global warming in a meadow.
He stares into open space,
waiting for his owner,
to kiss his face.

EMPTY

My wallet is empty.
Veins within body are dry,
flaking and punctured,
in a desert without any juice,
waiting for forgiveness,
dreaming of a new start.
Pain penetrating the brain,
as if there is no hope,
trying to reach the peak,
with no footholds on the way up.
A slide coming straight down,
to playground without the laughs.
The emptiness echoes,
vibrating across the plain.
A dusty cloud in my mind.
Church bells ring,
swaying and trying hard,
but nothing is out there,
nothing at all.

PEACEFUL SURROUNDS

The quietness of the field,
echoing as if invisible.
I stand awash without thought,
in mud rising towards nakedness,
white legs obscured,
sinking without fear.
Peace and tranquillity,
making the quietness superior.
Humps in the uneven ground,
giving power to all around.
Trees looking and staring,
not a sound or a movement.
Leaves invisible and see-through,
unreal and looking dead.
The suppressed voices,
faking the sound,
movement non-existent.
The quietness of the field.

ROLE OF LIFE

Life is like a cloud.
A beast up in space.
Pigs flying without wings.
Ducks deprived of water.
I'm trying hard not to believe.
Brain withering emotionally,
wondering about its devotion.
Knowledge is critical.
Sight is not always genuine,
when looking through glasses.
What do I generally perceive?
Army flying into combat,
or a volcano erupting,
exploding when we argue,
cuddling when making up.
Imagination a major dilemma,
a poem I am trying to compose,
a storyteller with passion.
Looking up at the heavens,
clouds are my inspiration,
my feelings looking in.

THE MEMORIAL BENCH

Colour of oak gives it some panache,
majestic lion's feet for grandeur,
memorial plate for the memories.
I look at the sea below,
water gushing against the rocks,
noise relaxing the soul.
Remembering great holidays whilst alive,
happiness looking back and smiling.
When young embracing but not caring,
arguing as if the world had ended,
making up and grinning with excitement,
like a river flowing towards the sea.
Children playing hide and seek,
behind hedges hiding from the rest.
The old still pretending to be young,
cuddling close like teenagers.
I look at the sea in deep thought,
past, present and tomorrow the same.

BODY FLOATATIONS

Steam rising towards the sky,
erupting into space,
echoing towards the heavens,
body floating aloft.
Skin white and flaky,
alive in their minds,
waiting for the answer,
hauntings of the soul.
Whistling of the wind,
final frontier of life.
The gods are waiting.
Sinners wait in line,
clutching thoughts,
evil vices they regret.
Old ghosts hang around,
fresh bodies to assist.
Rigid and scared they become,
knowing dead they are
and forever they will be,
except once a day,
joined by other ghosts,
giving them time to play.

SCARF ON HEAD

Stopping wind from penetrating,
firing towards the head,
heater warming the brain,
burning the inner skull,
helping the thought process.
Protecting the eyelid,
stopping tears from flowing,
a quiet running stream.
Easing pain from lumpy cheeks,
reducing colour on the face,
stopping cracks and flakes,
insulating the body whole,
environmentally protecting all.
Scarf on the head,
never to be cold again.

THE BRAIN

Controlling panel of the brain,
a computer within ourselves.
Receptors reaching spinal cord,
tunnelling sperm cells mechanically,
electrical currents exploding,
lightning inside our body.
Then thunder erupting,
with nerve cords shattering,
receptors firing at speed,
signalling to our bodies to respond.
Making eyes focus on an enemy.
Ears to listen intensely.
Nose to smell the aromas.
Arms to strengthen muscles.
Hands to grab passionately.
Legs to run in any direction correctly.
All taking their instructions,
from our personal supervisor.
Responsibility is solely the brain's.

INTRUDER WITHIN

The heart is erupting,
body inside shaking and dreading,
unwanted guests are visiting,
squatters taking residence within,
but bills they are not paying.
Building castles for their protection,
fighting the human immune system,
using veins for transportation,
travelling swiftly between regions.
Cancer cells are the aggressors,
like Roman warriors invading,
no modern weapons of destruction.
Cells slowly dying, new ones fighting.
Defeated, blood fills compartments,
cancer cells will invade once more,
capturing a new territory,
forcing new veins to be their slaves.
Hope human immune system wins the war,
eventually killing the cancer cells.

STORM IN A TEACUP

Breeze fluffing the edge,
not recording a dilemma,
small but serious in mind,
brain punctured and flat.
Rewinding memories aloud,
shaking wand and expecting,
life's riddles will be resolved.
Answer will fill the psyche,
adult skin erupting into space.
Mind thinking without thought,
hoping dictionary will assist,
words and sentences will fill the page,
crisis will disappear without trace.
Hollow and empty feelings absorbed,
naked eerie, truth non-existent,
storm in a teacup evaporating.
A desert left behind.
A desert left behind.

INNER LIE

Words hide in a tunnel,
visible only to myself,
imagining as if true,
lying to my innermost soul.
Regrets I can't reveal,
though it's leaving my ragged skull.
Lyrics absconding into space,
rhythm and rhyme fading.
Stories controlling thought patterns;
murderer I need to conquer;
an agent cool and calculated;
lovers hot and close to the equator.
Narratives circling life's matter,
every phrase anguishing,
imprinted within my heart.
Fingers loose and muscular.
Manuscript departing laptop.
Publisher getting excited.
Editor taking control.
My baby escaping down a hole,
novel escaping through tunnel,
making it visible to read.

CPSIA information can be obtained
at www.ICGtesting.com
Printed in the USA
LVHW111306030822
724896LV00005B/102